Let's shake Hands

VIRTUE STORIES

Lalita Iyer

Om KIDZ
An imprint of Om Books International

Antony was never going to play with Krish again. He was so mad at him!

Every time they went cycling around the block, Krish liked to bump into Antony's cycle with his own. Last evening, it made Antony fall and he had scraped his knee badly.

'Enough of cycling. I am going to play table tennis instead,' Antony muttered to himself. He was still very mad!

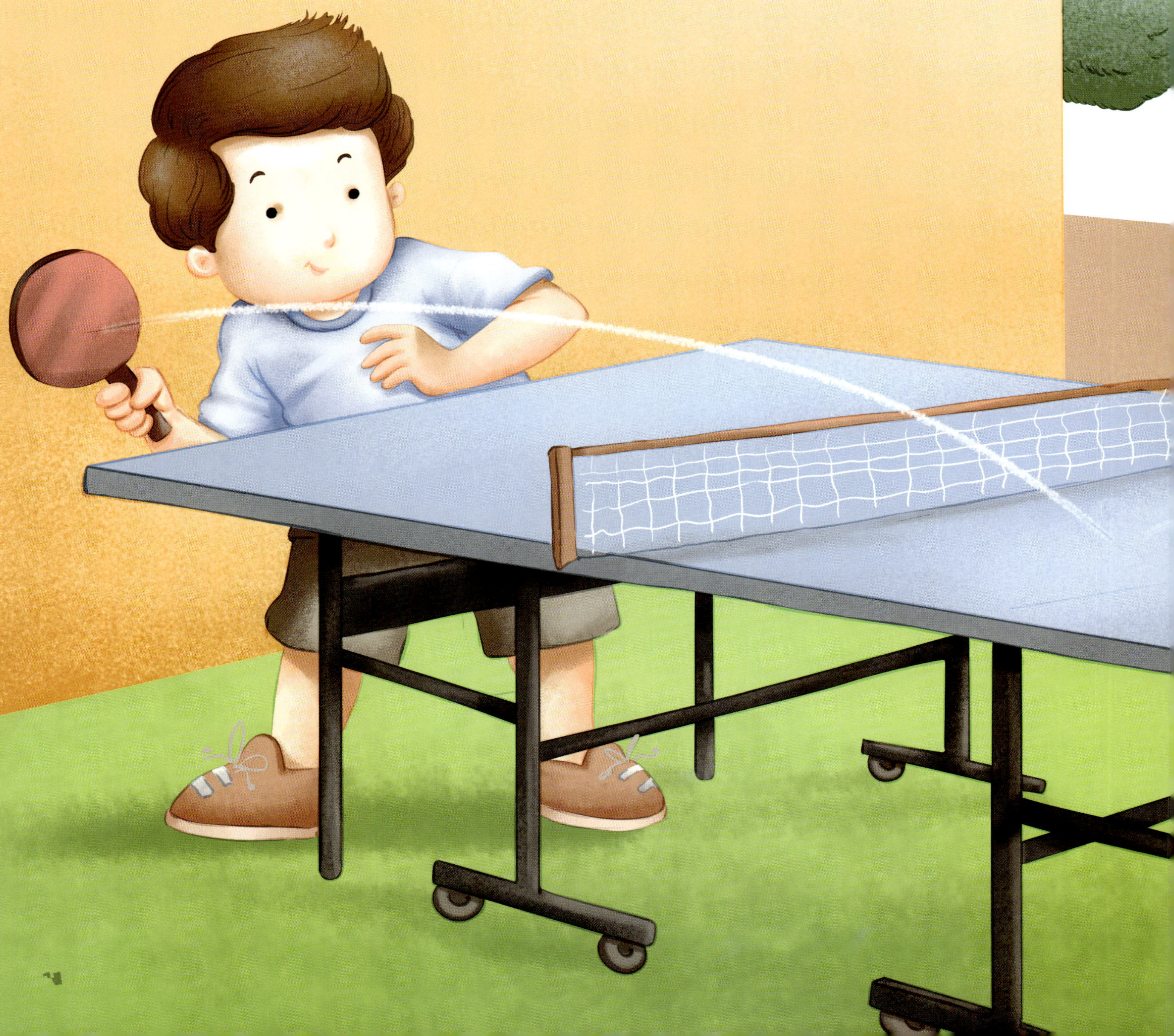

The next evening, Krish called out to him as he walked across to the table tennis table. Antony pretended not to hear. Krish cycled towards the table tennis table and waited for a chance as Antony played with another boy.

Antony won the game and seemed excited. Krish asked him, “Hey, can I play a game with you now?”.

But Antony said he was bored and moved on to the jungle gym. Krish ran after him and asked if they could play "Swing-Like-A-Jungle-Monkey" on the bars but Antony said he hated that game.

Krish was hurt and said nothing. He stood watching Antony swing on the bars.

Antony's mother, who was taking his baby sister for a walk in her pram, called him over. She had noticed Anthony was ill- tempered that day though he would not admit it. He was irritable. She asked him the reason for his behaviour.

'Because he always bumps my cycle hard with his cycle. I don't like it. So I don't want to play with him,' Antony muttered angrily.

His mother asked if Krish played nicely with him at other times. Antony thought for a moment. Then he said, 'yes.'

His mother said that perhaps Krish did not know that Antony did not like being bumped with his cycle.

'Why don't you tell him what you like and what you don't like? Maybe, you can still have fun playing together?'

'This way you can still be friends and agree to disagree nicely so both of you don't feel sad and grumpy either.' Antony's mom reasoned with him.

Antony thought about it for a few seconds earnestly. He then walked over to where Krish was hanging from one of the jungle gym bars,a sad look on his face.

'Don't bump my cycle with yours.
I don't like it.' Antony said.

'Oh, ok, I didn't know,' said Krish.
Antony stuck out his hand. Krish shook it.

A smile decorated their happy faces as they both played 'Swing-Like-A-Jungle-Monkey' for a while and later, cycled together.

This time, Krish was careful that he did not bump into Antony's cycle. Both decided that they would shake hands on anything they didn't like about each other in the future. They were good friends again!